# A First Myths Story Book

Myths and legends for the very young
from around the world

Stories retold by
## Mary Hoffman

Illustrated by
Roger Langton

Kevin Kimber

FENN PUBLISHING COMPANY LIMITED
www.hbfenn.com

# Contents

For Adam Lassiter

**A DK PUBLISHING BOOK**

**Project Editor** Naia Bray-Moffatt
**Art Editor** Catherine Goldsmith

**For Dorling Kindersley**
**Managing Editor** Dawn Sirett
**Managing Art Editor**
Sarah Wright-Smith
**Jacket Design** Claire Penny
**Production** Josie Alabaster

First published in Canada in 1999
by Fenn Publishing Company Ltd.
34 Nixon Road, Bolton,
Ontario, L7E 1W2

Visit us on the World Wide Web at www.hbfenn.com

Fenn Publishing Company Limited, Toronto, Canada

Copyright © 1999 Dorling Kindersley Limited, London

Text Copyright © 1999 Mary Hoffman

Published in Great Britain by
Dorling Kindersley Limited.

Cataloguing in Publication Information is available
from the National Library of Canada.
ISBN 1-55168-213-3

Reproduced by Bright Arts of Hong Kong
Printed and bound in Italy by Graphicom

The publishers would like to thank A.P. Watt Ltd on
behalf of The Trustees of the Robert Graves Copyright
Trust for permission to credit *The Greek Myths* by
Robert Graves as a source of reference.

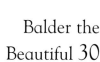

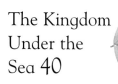

# Introduction

What's the difference between a myth and a legend? Myths are stories invented by people thousands of years ago to explain what they could see around them. In myths, gods and goddesses create the earth, sky, and oceans. They put the sun, moon, and stars in the sky and people and animals on earth. But they act like ordinary people too, having quarrels and feeling sad and throwing tantrums, which explains events like the changing seasons, storms and earthquakes, floods and volcanoes.

Then there are legends: stories about heroes and monsters, journeys to enchanted worlds, and the foundation of great cities. Legends are almost as fantastic as myths, but may have grown from something that really once happened, which changed and became more elaborate as more and more people told the story.

Just because the stories are mostly made up, it doesn't mean that myths and legends can't tell us truths. In this book, there are some that show us bad things about being human, like envy, greed, and vanity. But other tales tell us about the good side – love, bravery, and friendship. And these qualities are still as much a part of our daily lives as they were thousands of years ago.

# The Fall of Icarus

Daedalus the inventor was being held prisoner on the island of Crete with his son Icarus. King Minos was guarding all the harbors so that they couldn't escape by sea.

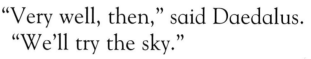

"Very well, then," said Daedalus. "We'll try the sky."

He meant they would fly away from the island like birds. Daedalus gathered up all the feathers he could. Then he tied them together and stuck them in place with wax to make two pairs of wings.

"Now you can fly," said Daedalus, strapping the wings to Icarus's arms, "but there are some important rules. Stay close behind me and we will get home safely. Don't fly too high or the sun will melt the wax. And don't fly too low or the sea will make your feathers soggy."

They climbed to the top of a cliff
and leaped off, soaring like eagles.

At first Icarus stayed close to his father,
but soon he was having too much fun to
remember the rules. He rose higher
and higher in the sky . . .

. . . closer and closer to the hot sun.

When Daedalus looked back he
couldn't see Icarus. He called out
his name, but there was no reply.

Daedalus spotted a few feathers
floating on the waves below. Then
he realized the wings had failed
and Icarus had fallen into the sea.

# The Golden Touch

Silenus the satyr had gotten lost. To tell the truth, he had had too much to drink and had fallen asleep in a garden, so his companions couldn't find him. They had gone home without him.

King Midas found the satyr sleeping in the palace rose garden. "You can stay here with me if you like," he said.

Silenus was a great storyteller and kept Midas and his court amused with his tales for five days.

Then the satyr said, "I should go home. My master, Dionysus, will be wondering where I am."

So Midas took Silenus back to the god Dionysus, who was very pleased to see him.

6

"You have looked after him well, Midas," said the god. "What present can I give you to show my thanks?"

"I would like everything I touch to turn to gold," said Midas. "Then in a very short time I will be rich beyond my wildest dreams."

Dionysus granted his wish. As Midas walked home, he had great fun turning flowers and stones to gold.

And everything he touched in his palace turned to gold too! "Ha ha!" laughed Midas. "Now I will be the richest man in the world!"

Midas was thirsty after his journey. His wine cup turned to gold, but then, so did his wine as soon as it touched his lips. Not one drop of liquid reached his throat. It was solid gold.

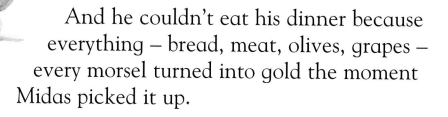

And he couldn't eat his dinner because everything – bread, meat, olives, grapes – every morsel turned into gold the moment Midas picked it up.

Now, King Midas had a little daughter, his favorite person in the whole world. She came running to greet him.

"Daddy, I'm so glad you're home," she cried, and before Midas could stop her she rushed into his arms. Instantly, she became a gold statue of a little girl.

Midas realized how greedy and foolish he had been. Weeping, he went back to Dionysus and begged him to take the golden touch away. The god saw that King Midas had learned his lesson.

He told the king to wash in a special river and promised that the gift would be washed away in the water.

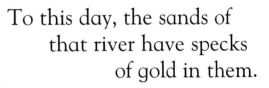

To this day, the sands of that river have specks of gold in them.

King Midas came home to find his child flesh and blood once again. "I am rich indeed," said Midas as he embraced her.

# Andromeda

There was a queen of Ethiopia named Cassiopeia. She was very beautiful, and she had an equally beautiful daughter, named Andromeda.

"My darling," said the queen. "Just look at us! We are so lovely that I think we must be even prettier than the sea nymphs."

The queen's palace was on the coast, and her words soon reached the sea nymphs. They were very indignant. "Prettier than us? What nonsense!" they cried. "This mortal must be put in her place!"

There were fifty sea nymphs, the Nereids, and they all went to complain to their protector, the mighty sea god Poseidon. He couldn't refuse fifty angry and beautiful sea nymphs.

"The queen shall be punished," he promised.

Poseidon summoned up a terrifying sea monster and sent it to the coast of Ethiopia.

The people of Ethiopia were terrified. They couldn't fish or go out in their trading ships, because the monster sank their boats and ate the sailors. They went to King Cepheus and begged him to do something.

"My dear," said the king to the queen. "This monster is a punishment for your boasting. We must find out what the gods want us to do to put things right."

But when the king did find out, he wept bitter tears. The only way to get rid of the monster was to let it have the lovely Princess Andromeda.

Andromeda was chained to some rocks and waited for the monster to come and devour her. And it was surely going to.

But, as luck
would have
it, the hero
Perseus was flying
past the coast of Ethiopia
at just that moment. He spotted
the princess chained to the rocks and
saw the serpent rushing toward her. Then
he swooped down to the water.

With one swift blow, Perseus cut off the monster's
head and Andromeda was saved. Perseus and
Andromeda were married. The monster had given
Cassiopeia such a fright that she never boasted again.

And all of them – the king, the queen,
Princess Andromeda, and
Perseus – were placed in the
heavens when they died.
You can still see the stars
named after them in
the night sky.

# Wolf Babies

In ancient Italy, there were twin little boys who had a very strange family. Their real mother was a princess named Sylvia, and their father was Mars, the great war god.

When Sylvia gave birth to the twin boys, her uncle Amulius was furious.

Amulius had stolen his kingdom from Sylvia's father, and he didn't want her sons to get it back when they were older. So Amulius had Sylvia and her two sons thrown into a river.

Sylvia was rescued by a river god, but the twins were swept away.

The swift stream carried the babies' cradle far away. The waters rushed into the Tiber River, which overflowed its banks.

The little boys were washed ashore under a fig tree. They were hungry and started to cry. A she wolf had come down to the water to drink. When she heard the babies crying, she lifted them gently out of their cradle and carried them back to her den.

There the twin boys drank their wolf mother's milk and grew up with wolf brothers and sisters.

When they got older, the two boys were adopted by shepherds, who named them Romulus and Remus.

The twins found out that they came from a king's family, and both wanted to build a city on the banks of the Tiber River. But they couldn't agree on the right place to start building. Romulus wanted one hill, and Remus preferred another.

So a competition was held to see who should build the city . . . and Romulus won. Remus was jealous of his brother.

He waited until Romulus had started to build the wall of his city . . .

. . . then he jumped over the wall.

"Hey, Romulus!" he said. "It's going to be really easy to invade your city! So much for your defenses!"

Romulus was furious with Remus for making fun of him. He knocked him to the ground, and the two brothers had the most tremendous fight – which Romulus won.

"My city is going to be the most beautiful the world has ever seen," he panted. "And the strongest!"

And Romulus was right. The city he built was called Rome. And you can still visit it today.

17

# Coyote Dances with a Star

Coyote was very full of himself. He thought he could do anything he liked.

One day he took it into his head that he would like to dance with a star.

So he called to a star, "Hey, come down here. I want to dance with you!" And the star descended gracefully through the sky.

They danced and danced until Coyote's legs were tired and his arms ached from hanging onto the star.

"I want to stop now," he said. "Put me down." But he wouldn't wait until the star was close to the earth.

He just let go and fell to the ground – splat!

Luckily for Coyote, he had more than one life. It took a while, but one day he was back to normal. And he started looking at stars again. There was one near his lodge, with a beautiful long tail.

"Hey, come down and dance with me," said Coyote. And the star descended. Coyote grabbed hold of the tail and the star was off again, whirling through the sky.

But it went so fast that Coyote started to come apart. Bits of him dropped off and fell to earth. It was a good thing Coyote had more than one life!

But this time, when he got back to normal, he had learned his lesson. "You win," he said to the Great Mystery that rules the universe. "No more dancing with stars."

# The First Corn

At the beginning of time, there was a man who lived on his own. He had nothing to eat but roots and nuts and berries. And he didn't know how to make fire, so all his food was cold and raw.

The man was very sad and lonely. He curled up in the sunshine and slept the days away. When he woke up, he saw a beautiful woman with long fair hair quite unlike his own. At first he was afraid.

But then he realized he didn't have to be lonely any more. He sang to the woman about how sad he was on his own. "Stay with me," he begged. "Do as I say, and I shall be with you forever," the woman replied.

She led him to some dry grass and showed him how to start a fire by rubbing two sticks together. Soon a spark flew out and the grass caught fire.

Before long, a large patch of land was completely cleared. "Wait until sundown," said the woman. "Then take me by the hair and drag me over the ground." The man didn't want to, but he did as she asked.

"In the spring, there will be plants wherever you dragged me," she said. "And you will see my hair spilling out between the leaves."

# A Newborn Warrior

Coatlicue was the earth goddess of old Mexico. She had four hundred sons, who were the stars in the southern sky. And she had one daughter, Coyolxauqui, the goddess of the night.

One day, when Coatlicue was sweeping the floor, she found a ball of feathers. She picked it up and tucked it neatly into the waistband of her skirt of snakes.

But Coatlicue didn't know that the ball of feathers contained a powerful magic.

It was not long before Coatlicue realized she was expecting another baby. She had no idea that it was because of the magic ball of feathers.

When Coatlicue told her children what was happening to her, they became very angry.

"You are too old for this sort of thing," said Coyolxauqui. "Tell us who is the father of your child."

But Coatlicue couldn't tell her because she didn't know. All her sons were angry with her too.

In the end, Coyolxauqui was so furious with her mother that she chased her out of the house.

Coatlicue ran away from her home
and along the mountain paths.
But her children were all
following her, shouting
and waving weapons.
"What shall I do?"
moaned Coatlicue.

Then things got worse, because as
Coatlicue reached the top of Coatepec
Mountain, she felt a bad pain.
"The baby is coming,"
she cried.

She lay down on
the ground and
gave birth –
not to a baby,
but to a fully
armed warrior.

His skin was
blue and gold,
and he carried a
flaming sword.

His name was Huitzilopochtli, and he was, in fact, the sun.

He leaped to his mother's defense because her other children were trying to kill her.

In spite of being newly born, he killed his sister, the goddess of the night, and most of his star brothers.

The other brothers ran away and hid in the South.

And so it happens every morning that the sun puts the night and stars to flight.

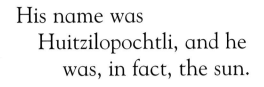

25

# How the Animals Got Their Shapes

This is how animals began in Australia: first they were hidden in the frozen earth. Then the sun goddess, Yhi, warmed them into life. But they didn't like the kinds of lives they had been given.

The animals that lived in the water wanted to be on land. And the ones on land wanted to be in the sky.

They grew so sad that Yhi came down from the heavens to see what was the matter.

"Now everything will be all right," they said. "Yhi will give us new shapes."

"Tell me what is wrong," said Yhi.

All the animals spoke at once making a
terrible racket. But at last Yhi
got them to make their
requests one at a time. "I
would like legs," said Lizard.
"I'm tired of wriggling through the water."

"And I would like wings,"
said Bat, "so I can fly
through the air like a bird."

"Big back legs for me," said Kangaroo,
"and a long tail to balance me when I leap."

"I want longer legs too," said Pelican,
"so my belly doesn't get wet when I'm
fishing. And a bag to keep fish in."

Yhi granted all their wishes,
which is why Australian
animals look the way
they do today.

# How Butterflies Began

Long ago, before there were any people in Australia, the animals could talk. They had never known death, but one day a young cockatoo fell out of a high tree and broke his neck.

"What's the matter with him?" asked the kookaburra. "He won't open his eyes." "Why doesn't he get up and fly away?" asked the wagtail.

No one could understand that the cockatoo was dead. Then the crow threw a stick into the river. It sank and rose again.

"That's what has happened to the cockatoo," said the crow. "He has gone to another world and will return."

Then all the animals volunteered to go to the other world. The opossum, wombat, and snake all hid for the winter. But when they woke up in the spring, they were just the same.

Then the insects tried it. All the caterpillars wrapped themselves up and hid in the bark of trees or under the ground.

When the next spring came, all the caterpillars had disappeared. Instead, the Australian countryside was full of butterflies – yellow, red, blue, and green.

"You've solved the mystery of death," said all the animals. "You've been to the other world and come back different and more beautiful."

# Balder the Beautiful

Balder was the most beautiful of all the Norse gods. He was the son of Odin, the chief god, and his wife, Frigg.

Balder had a blind brother named Hoder.

Frigg loved them both very much. But she was scared that something bad might happen to Balder, so she decided on a plan to keep him safe forever.

Frigg thought that if she asked everything in the whole world to promise never to hurt her beautiful son, Balder would never die.

The goddess Frigg traveled through the whole world, asking every plant and animal to promise never to hurt Balder. And she asked every stone the same. And every metal.

She asked fire and water and the four winds to make the same promise.

Frigg thought she had asked everything in the living world and every mineral not to hurt her precious son.

But Frigg had forgotten to ask one thing. It was a plant that didn't grow in the ground, the mistletoe, which grows on oak trees. By forgetting to speak to the mistletoe, Frigg made a terrible mistake.

The gods and goddesses had great fun when Frigg told them that nothing could hurt her son Balder. They gathered in the great hall of Odin's palace, Valhalla, and made a great pile of sharp and heavy weapons.

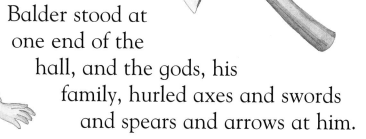

Balder stood at one end of the hall, and the gods, his family, hurled axes and swords and spears and arrows at him.

They threw furniture, too, and cups and bowls and burning firebrands. But everything fell harmlessly to the ground. Balder stood unhurt amid all the missiles because they were all made of things that kept their promise to Frigg.

Loki, a cunning and mean god, knew about the mistletoe. He cut a branch of it and sharpened the stem to a point, like a spear.

"Here, Hoder," he said to Balder's blind brother. "Wouldn't you like to join in the game? I can help you throw a weapon at Balder."

Hoder was happy to take a turn at the game all the other gods were enjoying so much. He let Loki put the weapon in his hand and help him throw it.

Loki's aim was perfect. The mistletoe dart pierced Balder's chest, and he fell down dead. Loki was punished, but his trick taught Odin that there were some things even a god couldn't control.

# Rama and Sita

When Dasharatha was king of Kosala in India, there was a terrible ten-headed monster ravaging the land. Ravana was his name, and King Dasharatha prayed to the gods to give him sons strong enough to kill the demon.

He had four sons by three different wives, but his favorite was Rama. Rama was the eldest, and his best friend was his half-brother Lakshmana.

Rama grew up strong and handsome, and he won for himself a beautiful princess named Sita.

Rama and Sita got married, and Lakshmana married Sita's sister. They were all very happy.

But it didn't last. King Dasharatha chose Rama to be his heir, but the mother of one of the other sons tricked the king into banishing Rama for fourteen years. Rama and Sita went to live in the forest, and Lakshmana chose to go with them.

They lived for ten years by a lake, and during this time Rama killed many demons. The news reached Ravana, who decided to punish Rama by stealing his wife.

Another demon disguised himself as a golden deer and went to visit Sita. As soon as she tried to stroke him, he leaped away.

Rama was suspicious. He left Sita with Lakshmana and went in search of the deer.

Rama shot the deer with his arrows, and as it died it cried out, "Help, Sita! Help, Lakshmana!" in Rama's own voice. Sita heard it and sent Lakshmana to go see what had happened to her husband.

At that moment Ravana struck. He carried Sita off. She dropped some jewels and her golden scarf where some very special monkeys found them.

Rama searched everywhere for Sita until one day he came to the palace of the monkey king. The king had a brave captain named Hanuman who helped Rama with his search.

Hanuman found Sita on the island of Lanka. His army of monkeys made a bridge to the island and swarmed across it.

There was a terrible battle, and after a long struggle Rama shot Ravana with his mighty bow.

Rama asked the gods to bring back to life all the monkeys who had died in the battle. And Rama and Sita were together again. Their long banishment was over, and they became king and queen of Kosala, never to be separated again.

# The Enchanted Island

There was a sailor in ancient Egypt who set out on a voyage. But before he had gone very far, a terrible storm blew up. The ship was wrecked, and everyone on board was drowned except this one sailor.

He was flung into the sea with all the other sailors, but luckily he found a bit of wood from the broken ship.

He clung to it for dear life until the storm calmed down.

At last he was washed up on the shore of an island. "May the gods be praised," he gasped, and then fell exhausted onto the sand. It was some days before he had enough strength to look for food.

He found that the island was full of fruit and the sea around it teemed with fish. He sat down to his first meal in days. But before he began to eat, he offered thanks to the gods. Immediately, there was a clap of thunder.

A huge serpent god towered over the sailor. "How did you get here?" asked the serpent. "Tell me the truth or you will die." The sailor told him truthfully about the shipwreck.

The god gave him gifts of treasure and said a ship would take him back to Egypt. "But the island will never be seen again," said the serpent. And it never was.

39

# The Kingdom Under the Sea

Hoderi was a great fisherman, and Hoori, his younger brother, was a clever hunter. One day, the two brothers decided to swap weapons.

So Hoderi took Hoori's bow and arrows, and Hoori took his brother's fishhook. They agreed to meet at the end of the day and tell each other their adventures.

But it seemed as if there wouldn't be much to tell, because both brothers were unlucky.

Hoori caught not one single fish all day. And, what was worse, he dropped his brother's fishhook into the water. "What am I going to do?" he said. "Hoderi is going to be so angry with me."

Hoderi came back from his day's hunting in a bad mood. "Hunting is stupid," he said. "I didn't catch anything. Give me back my hook!" He was very upset when Hoori told him the hook was lost.

Hoderi refused to have any other hook. So Hoori was lowered into the sea in a basket to search for the missing one.

He soon found himself at the bottom of the ocean, in the palace of the sea god.

Hoori asked all the fish if they had seen Hoderi's hook. At last, he found one who had it in her mouth.

Of course, Hoori should have gone back then, but he met the beautiful daughter of the sea god.

Toyotama was her name, and she was as lovely as a cherry blossom.

But both Toyotama and her father could change into water dragons whenever they wanted.

Hoori and Toyotama were married and lived so happily together that Hoori forgot all about returning the fishhook. And he forgot his brother, Hoderi, too.

After three years, Hoori suddenly remembered his brother and decided he would return to land and give the hook back to Hoderi.

Toyotama was sad. "I shall come and find you, Hoori," she said. "For I am going to bear your child."

Hoori kissed her good-bye and swam to the surface.

How happy Hoderi was to see his brother again! "I thought you had been drowned years ago," he said.

Princess Toyotama came to the shore and gave birth to a baby boy. Then she turned into a dragon and returned to her kingdom under the sea. Hoori's son became the father of the first emperor of Japan.

# The Crocodile and the Baby

Three women were washing clothes in the river when two of them decided to play a trick on the third. They hid their babies in the rushes, and then said, "We have thrown our babies into the river. Why don't you do the same?"

The third woman untied her baby from her back and threw it into the water.

Immediately, along swam a huge crocodile that swallowed the baby in one gulp.

The two cruel women laughed, but the baby's mother tore her hair with grief. "I will get my baby back," she cried. She decided to climb the Paradise tree to ask the great spirit Mulungu for help.

She climbed and climbed until she was above the clouds. There she met a tribe of beautiful leopards. They let her pass because she was polite to them.

On she climbed, past birds and fish, until in the end she reached the great spirit Mulungu.

At the very top of the tree, she told her story. "Please give my baby back," she begged. And Mulungu was so impressed by her goodness and love for her baby that he summoned the crocodile and made it return the baby.

The mother was very happy, and so was her baby. The only sad one was the crocodile.

# Who's Who in First Myths

## Andromeda    Page 10
Ethiopian princess. The beautiful daughter of Cassiopeia, she was saved by Perseus from being eaten by a sea monster. *Greek legend.*

## Balder    Page 30

Norse god. He was the son of Odin and Frigg and was accidentally killed by his blind brother, Hoder. *Norse myth.*

## Cassiopeia    Page 10
Queen of Ethiopia. The mother of Andromeda, she was punished for being vain. *Greek legend.*

## Coatlicue    Page 22
Aztec earth goddess. She was the mother of Coyolxauqui, Huitzilopochtli, and four hundred other sons. *Aztec myth.*

## Coyolxauqui    Page 22

Aztec goddess of the night. She was killed by her half-brother, Huitzilopochtli. *Aztec myth.*

## Coyote    Page 18
The trickster figure in the mythology of several Native American peoples. *N. American myth.*

## Daedalus    Page 4
Greek inventor and architect who built the labyrinth for King Minos on Crete. Father of Icarus. *Greek legend.*

## Dasharatha    Page 34
King of Kosala in India. Father of Rama, Lakshmana, and their two brothers. *Hindu legend.*

## Dionysus    Page 6
Greek god of feasting and drinking. Patron of Silenus. *Greek myth/legend.*

## Frigg    Page 30
Norse goddess. Married to Odin, the chief god. Mother of Balder and Hoder. *Norse myth.*

## Hanuman    Page 34
Very clever and brave monkey. Captain of the monkey king's army in the story of Rama and Sita. *Hindu legend.*

## Hoder    Page 30
Blind brother of Balder. Son of Frigg and Odin. *Norse myth.*

## Hoderi    Page 40
Great Japanese fisherman. Brother of Hoori. *Japanese legend.*

## Hoori    Page 40
Great Japanese hunter. Brother of Hoderi. He married the daughter of the sea god. *Japanese legend.*

## Huitzilopochtli    Page 22
Aztec sun god. Son of Coatlicue. *Aztec myth.*

## Icarus    Page 4
Son of Daedalus. He died trying to fly with wings made by his father. *Greek legend.*

## Lakshmana     Page 34
Half-brother of Rama.
*Hindu legend.*

## Loki     Page 30

An immortal not accepted by the other Norse gods. He played tricks, including the one that killed Balder. *Norse myth.*

## Mars     Page 14
Roman god of war. Father of Romulus and Remus.
*Roman legend.*

## Midas     Page 6
Greek king who was famous for being rich.
*Greek myth/legend.*

## Minos     Page 4
King of Crete. He commissioned Daedalus to build a labyrinth to hide the Minotaur, a creature that was half-man, half-bull. Then Minos would not let Daedalus leave Crete.
*Greek legend.*

## Mulungu     Page 44
African sky spirit, who gave back a woman's baby after it had been swallowed by a crocodile.
*Chaga legend.*

## Odin     Page 30
Chief of the Norse gods. Father of Balder and Hoder. *Norse myth.*

## Perseus     Page 10
Greek hero. He rescued Andromeda from the sea monster.
*Greek legend.*

## Poseidon     Page 10
Greek god of the sea. He sent the sea monster to punish Cassiopeia for being vain. *Greek legend.*

## Rama     Page 34
Hero of the Hindu epic *The Ramayana*. He was married to Sita. *Hindu legend.*

## Ravana     Page 34

A ten-headed demon who stole Sita from Rama. *Hindu legend.*

## Remus     Page 14
Son of Mars and Sylvia. His twin brother was Romulus, who founded the city of Rome. *Roman legend.*

## Romulus     Page 14
Twin brother of Remus. He founded the city of Rome. *Roman legend.*

## Silenus     Page 6
Satyr, a goat-legged creature of Greek mythology, who loved to tell stories.
*Greek myth/legend.*

## Sita     Page 34
Indian princess. She was the wife of Rama. She was captured by Ravana the demon and rescued by Rama, his half-brother, and a troop of brave monkeys.
*Hindu legend.*

## Sylvia     Page 14
(also called Rhea Sylvia and Ilia) Mother of Romulus and Remus. She was cast into a river by her uncle and saved by a river god.
*Roman legend.*

## Toyotama     Page 40
Princess of the kingdom under the sea. She could turn into a dragon at will. She married Hoori, a mortal, and bore him a son.
*Japanese legend.*

## Yhi     Page 26
Aborigine sun goddess. She gave Australian animals their strange shapes.
*Aborigine myth.*

# About the Stories

I have lots of books of myths and legends on my shelves and am also a great user of libraries and the internet. But some of the stories in this book I have known since I was a little girl – the death of Balder is the first story I remember being told. If you and your child want to find out more about each story, here are some other books you might try reading.
M.H.

The Fall of Icarus, The Golden Touch, and Andromeda
A good sourcebook for all Greek myths and legends is
*Greek Myths* by Robert Graves (Penguin complete edition, 1992)

Wolf Babies
There is no convenient source for the well-known story of Romulus and Remus,
which comes from several Greek and Roman writers. I have used the scholarly
work *Remus* by T.P. Wiseman (Cambridge University Press, 1995)

Coyote Dances with a Star
*American Indian Myths and Legends*
by Richard Erdoes and Alfonso Ortiz (Pantheon, 1984)

The First Corn
*Tales of the North American Indians* by Stith Thompson
(Indiana University Press, 1929)

A Newborn Warrior
*Aztec and Maya Myths* by Karl Taube (British Museum Press, 1993)

How the Animals Got Their Shapes
This is based on a story in *Myths and
Legends of Australia* by A.W. Reed (Reed, 1965)

How Butterflies Began
*Aborigine Myths and Legends* by William Ramsay Smith
(Senate, 1996. Originally published 1930)

Balder the Beautiful
The main source for Norse myths and legends is *Prose Edda*
by Snorri Sturlusson. A convenient modern retelling is *The Norse Myths*
by Kevin Crossley-Holland (André Deutsch, 1980)

Rama and Sita
The Hindu epic *The Ramayana* is a long tale, filling four volumes in the
original. I have relied on *Indian Tales and Legends* by J.E.B. Gray
(Oxford University Press, 1989)

The Enchanted Island
*Egyptian Myth and Legend* by Donald A. Mackenzie (Gresham)

The Kingdom Under the Sea
*Myths and Legends of Japan* by F. Hadland Davis
(Dover paperback, 1992)

The Crocodile and the Baby
This is based on a story in *African-American Alphabet* by Gerald Hausman
(St. Martin's Press Inc., 1997)